BOG

THE CIT

Edificio Ba
Skidmore, Ow
Lever House as the template when assisting
on the design of this 1960 tower.
Carrera 10a y 14

Santuario Monserrate
Bogota may sit 2,500m 'closer to the stars',
but its religious retreat is even loftier.
See p014

Edificio Avianca
This 1969 tower by Germán Samper opened
the door for Downtown's first skyscrapers.
Parque Santander

Avenida Jiménez
Rogelio Salmona's water-themed intervention
follows the path of the old San Francisco river.

Universidad de los Andes
Felipe González's sports block and Guillermo
and Daniel Bermúdez's restored jail set the
tone for an architecturally eclectic campus.
See p078

Museo del Oro
Samper's 1968 gold museum is a must-see.
Nearby is the Condominio Parque Santander,
a delightfully geometric study in brick.
See p026

Banco de la República
Traditionalist Alfredo Rodríguez took some
flak in 1954 for his modern design. Formalist
firm Cuellar Serrano Gómez added the finesse.
Avenida Jiménez y 7

La Candelaria
In the city's historic centre, churches and
museums meet modern gems such as the
Biblioteca Luis Ángel Arango (see p068).

INTRODUCTION
THE CHANGING FACE OF THE URBAN SCENE

In less than a decade, Colombia has transformed itself from no-go to must-go, from a near failed state to one of endless optimism. It's easy to be impressed by Bogota's cultural outpouring, or inspired by the municipal 'urban temples' – library complexes built in deprived areas. Investors have piled into the capital, building a new airport, hotels and infrastructure to handle four million visitors a year. A convention centre by Spanish architects Herreros and local Daniel Bermúdez is due in 2014, which, together with a block by Steven Holl at the Universidad Nacional (see p074) and a cultural complex by Foster + Partners, will provide contemporary icons for a city proud of its nickname – the Athens of South America.

There are still problems; chronic congestion, corruption and an ongoing security situation, but they are nothing compared to the bombs and unbridled violence of the past. Colombia is on a quest to bury the *mala fama* (bad rep) that comes with being the world's largest cocaine producer. 'We make it, you take it,' is the retort from those tired of being blamed for others' vices. For years, travellers who chose to ignore the government warnings reaped the rewards from some of the world's friendliest and most beautiful people. And in the push to replace stereotypes, you too will be met by a charm offensive. Bogota is a success story of epic proportions in a thriving country that has an important lesson to share with the world. Go see for yourself. Just get there before everyone else.

ESSENTIAL INFO
FACTS, FIGURES AND USEFUL ADDRESSES

TOURIST OFFICE
Carrera 8 y 9-83
T 283 7115
www.bogotaturismo.gov.co

TRANSPORT
Car hire
Avis
T 629 1722
www.avis.com
Helicopter
Helicol
Via Catam, Entrada 6
T 594 0270
www.helicol.com.co
Taxis
Radio Taxi
T 288 8888
It's safest to call a cab or get
one at an official rank
TransMilenio
www.transmilenio.gov.co
Buses run from 5am to 12.15am; Sundays
and holidays, 6am to 11.15pm

EMERGENCY SERVICES
Emergencies
T 123
24-hour pharmacy
Farmatodo
Carrera 11 y 82-71, Local 1
T 743 2100

EMBASSIES
British Embassy
Carrera 9 y 76-49, Piso 8
T 326 8300
www.ukincolombia.fco.gov.uk
US Embassy
Calle 24 y 48-50
T 275 2000
bogota.usembassy.gov

POSTAL SERVICES
Post office
Servicios Postales Nacionales 4-72
Carrera 24 y 66a-30
T 419 9299
Shipping
DHL
Calle 72 y 10-70, Local 103p
T 742 3928
www.dhl.com.co

BOOKS
Delirium by Laura Restrepo (Vintage)
News of a Kidnapping by
Gabriel García Márquez (Penguin)
Paul Beer (La Silueta Ediciones)

WEBSITES
Architecture
www.a57.org
www.fundacionrogeliosalmona.org
Newspaper
www.eltiempo.com

EVENTS
ArtBO
www.artboonline.com
Iberoamericano de Teatro de Bogota
www.festivaldeteatro.com.co

COST OF LIVING
**Taxi from El Dorado International
Airport to city centre**
COP19,500
Cappuccino
COP3,500
Packet of cigarettes
COP4,000
Daily newspaper
COP1,800
Bottle of champagne
COP330,000

BOGOTA
Population
8 million
Currency
Colombian peso
Telephone codes
Colombia: 57
Bogota: 1
Local time
GMT -5
Flight time
London: 14 hours 30 minutes

Havana
Mexico City
San Juan
Caracas
Bogota
COLOMBIA
Lima
Brasilia

AVERAGE TEMPERATURE / °C

	J	F	M	A	M	J	J	A	S	O	N	D
40												
30												
20												
10												
00												
-10												
-20												

AVERAGE RAINFALL / MM

	J	F	M	A	M	J	J	A	S	O	N	D
120												
100												
080												
060												
040												
020												
000												

NEIGHBOURHOODS

THE AREAS YOU NEED TO KNOW AND WHY

To help you navigate the city, we've chosen the most interesting districts (see below and the map inside the back cover) and colour-coded our featured venues, according to their location; those venues that are outside these areas are not coloured.

EL RETIRO/ZONA T

A pedestrian area next to the Centro Andino mall (see p080), Zona T is the centre of gravity for a lively bar and club scene. High-end retailers are increasingly moving in but you can still have a right-old knees-up at Andrés Carne de Res (Calle 82 y 12-21, T 863 7880) or El Coq (see p039).

CIUDAD SALITRE

Bogota's green lung encompasses many of its major sports facilities and the sprawling campus of the Universidad Nacional (see p074). A new business district on Avenida El Dorado has pulled commerce here but the office crowd still prefer to head north to eat and drink when they knock off.

DOWNTOWN

In this bustling down-at-heel district you'll find what's left of the city's food markets; these days more likely to be peddling fake goods. To the north is Torre Colpatria (see p011), still Colombia's tallest building. Private artists' studios such as Las Nieves (see p082) are breathing new life into the centre, but don't bother after dark.

ZONA G/CHAPINERO

The English mansions of Quinta Camacho have been converted into the city's finest hotels (see p017), restaurants (see p056) and bars, in the area now known as Zona Gourmet (Zona G). A cooler crowd of artists and designers hang to the east of La Septima in Chapinero Alto's hip joints.

LA CANDELARIA

The historic centre laid out by the Spanish in the 16th century stretches for 10 blocks between the path of two former rivers, now Calle 6 and Calle 33. Some great contemporary architecture, such as the Biblioteca Luis Ángel Arango (see p068), has been woven into the colonial fabric.

PARQUE 93/CHICO NORTE

Designer hotels have gathered close to the offices of Colombia's big businesses. As you'd expect, there are plenty of places to eat, drink and socialise — one of the best is live-music venue Gaira Café Cumbia House (Carrera 13 y 96-11, T 746 2696), a piece of the Caribbean coast in Bogota.

LA MACARENA

Tucked into the hills east and north of the city's most strategic junction — Carrera 7 and Calle 26 — this boho barrio has some of the best one-off galleries, shops and eateries in town. The Torres del Parque (see p012) put La Macarena and Bosque Izquierdo on the map in the 1970s and the area has attracted creatives ever since.

TEUSAQUILLO/LA SOLEDAD

A Tudor fetish among Bogota's elite created this incongruous district in the early 20th century. For decades, Teusaquillo suffered from neglect but architects and artists are now moving in. The leafy avenues and International Style residences (see p077) of neighbouring La Soledad are also popular.

LANDMARKS
THE SHAPE OF THE CITY SKYLINE

Seen from Cerro de Monserrate (see p014), Bogota's urban sprawl is intimidating, but if you stay near the mountains, it's manageable. Traffic moves (or crawls) north-south on carreras, which rise in number the further west you head from the lush backdrop – almost everything you need is crammed into the strip between Carrera 1 and 14. Calles (streets) traverse east-west, their numbers increasing with the disposable income as you head north. The colonial core La Candelaria remains the administrative and cultural centre, and, facing it, Downtown is where you'll find the city's first cluster of skyscrapers, many of which were built in the 1960s. The best of these are Germán Samper's Mies-inspired Edificio Avianca (Parque Santander), the group of high-rises that form the original financial hub Centro Internacional (see p015) and the residential Torres del Parque (see p012), by Franco-Colombian maestro Rogelio Salmona.

The 1948 Bogotazo riots, which razed swathes of the centre, marked a turning point in the city's development. Fearful of a repeat, Bogota's money began to flee north, to Chapinero, Quinta Camacho, Nogales and La Cabrera. Restaurants, retail and hotels followed, and growth continues to creep further north to this day. High-end entertainment areas Zona G (Calle 68 y 5), Zona T (Calle 82 y 11) and Parque 93 (Calle 93 y 11) have attracted the lion's share of the recent boom and are landmarks of the Bogota night. *For full addresses, see Resources.*

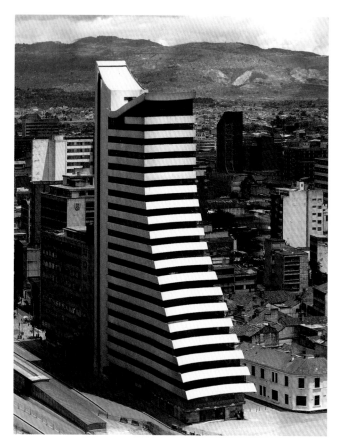

Edificio Aseguradora del Valle

Designed by architects ARK, this 70m-tall, Dalek-like tower went up in 1972 for a Cali insurance company wanting to make a mark in the capital. That it did. Indeed, the next-door Torre Colpatria (opposite) even rotated the monochromatic theme seven years later. The reason for Aseguradora's arching design was not simply a desire to make an impression on the skyline, but an attempt to open up offices on the northern facade to the sun. At ground level sits *La Rebeca*, Bogota's first nude statue; Hernando Henao Buriticá's marble figure caused quite the scandal in 1928. Much to the purists' chagrin, the emblematic Edificio Aseguradora spawned copycats across the country, notably in Barranquilla where the 'Miss Universe' building adopts a yet more capricious approach.
Carrera 10 y 24-55

Torre Colpatria

An amnesty on the repatriation of ill-gotten capital fuelled a race for the skies in the 1970s, and Cuellar Serrano Gómez's 190m Centro de Comercial Internacional (see p015) became Latin America's tallest building in 1977. Two years later, Obregón Valenzuela y Cía threw another 6m on to their stripy phallus to claim the prize. At 196m, the 49-storey Torre Colpatria, at the axis of two major thoroughfares, has reigned ever since, although construction began in 2011 on the proposed 240m BD Bacatá (Calle 19 y 5-20), by Barcelona firm Alonso Balaguer. To resist seismic activity, Colpatria required 50m of foundations and a skeleton of 28 concrete columns. A light show added in 1998 won a few friends for this unloved landmark; a viewing area is open at the weekend (T 283 6665).
Carrera 9 y 25

Torres del Parque

This trio of organic, spiralling brick stalagmites by Rogelio Salmona is one of the triumphs of Latin American architecture. Built from 1965 to 1970, the spacious, beautifully proportioned apartments, with their clever stepped balconies, are still in high demand 40 years later. Salmona lived in Torre B (pictured, right) until his death in 2007.
Carrera 5 y 26

Santuario Monserrate

On top of Cerro de Monserrate, 3,152m above sea level, this church has been a landmark since 1657. The original chapel was destroyed by an earthquake in 1917 and replaced three years later by a neo-colonial version which, although it might lack architectural allure, draws legions of visitors. They come for the wood sculpture of Jesus, carved in 1656 by Pedro de Lugo Albarracín, and the fantastic views. An alarming number of sinners climb 514m on their knees up through the eucalyptus trees to share Jesus' suffering and beg for miracles – you're better off getting the cable car (Carrera 1 y Avenida Circunvalar). Warm up with a chicken *ajiaco* (stew) at Casa Santa Clara (T 243 8952), a French-style mansion built in Usaquén in 1924 and hauled up the mountain in 1979. *www.cerromonserrate.com*

Edificio Bavaria

Architects Obregón Valenzuela y Cía's 24-storey tower (above, right) for Bavaria, the brewing company that made Julio Mario Santo Domingo Colombia's richest man, was completed in 1965 to great acclaim. The austere geometrical concrete high-rise, which raises a glass or two to NYC's Seagram Building, delivered a final flourish to Centro Internacional, construction of which began four years previously. Despite the lack of a masterplan, Bavaria sits in sync with Cuellar Serrano Gómez's Hotel and Residencias Tequendama and Edificio Bachué – although it's dwarfed by the concrete wedges of Centro de Comercial Internacional (behind) – and a warren of shops and restaurants links the buildings at ground level. Developers' plans to demolish the tower have not been well received.
Carrera 10 y 28

HOTELS

WHERE TO STAY AND WHICH ROOMS TO BOOK

Tax breaks offered in 2006 sparked a boom in hotel construction but it's still difficult to find the same high standards here as in, say, Mexico City or BA. Interior designer Miguel Soto upped the specs on the JW Marriott (Calle 73 y 8-60, T 481 6000) with tapestries by Olga de Amaral (see p030) and Jorge Lizarazo (see p086). The Hilton (Carrera 7 y 72-41, T 600 6100) also pulled out all the stops on its return to the city in 2011. Local operator BH Hoteles has a portfolio of urban retreats, the pick of which is the Mauricio Rojas-designed Parque 93 (Carrera 14 y 93a-69, T 743 2820), a black-brick tower. The impressive vertical garden facade of Hotel B3 (Carrera 15 y 88-36, T 691 8488) and Philip Weiss' rooftop pool at Cité Hotel (Carrera 15 y 88-10, T 646 7777) set them apart.

However, there were a clutch of exciting openings in 2012. The name is the only thing lacking allure at BOG (see p020), its location 'convenient' for Zona T and its design inspired by the country's natural treasures – gold and emeralds. Lizarazo provided plenty of flourish at the eco-friendly Hotel Bioxury (Calle 88 y 9-48), a tower a short stroll from the excellent traditional fare at Club Colombia (see p029). The 1950s home of the former mayor, Casa Gaitán Cortés (Calle 68 y 4-97, T 226 7247), has been cleverly converted into a hotel and the striking Plan B-designed Click-Clack (Carrera 11 y 93-77, T 691 9513) is faced by a huge map of the city. *For full addresses and room rates, see Resources.*

Casa Medina

Architect Santiago Medina created this building for his family from the rubble of two 16th- and 17th-century monasteries. It's a fascinating amalgamation of Spanish and French styles from 1946, featuring stone floors and columns, clay tiles and carved wood doors. To save it from the wrecking ball in the 1980s it was declared a national treasure and it's now Bogota's most historic stay outside La Candelaria, located just a stroll from Zona G. After a 2012 overhaul, an English feel is apparent in the 58 rooms – the Junior Suites (406, above) in the original eaves, furnished with Timothy Oulton's 'Kensington' sofas, are hugely atmospheric, but can be noisy. 'Secto' lamps by Seppo Koho, plasma TVs and iPads bring things bang up to date. *Carrera 7 y 69a-22, T 217 0288, www.hotelcharlestoncasamedina.com*

Sofitel Victoria Regia

If Bogota's troubled past puts you on edge, you'll feel nicely cocooned in the Victoria Regia, which has an army of staff flitting around the marbled lobby (above), providing faultless service under stained glass. The 1994 hotel was refreshed in 2012 by Miguel Soto, and the 102 high-spec rooms feature (some might say) a brave colour scheme of red, purple and blue; Junior Suites have the most space.

Sofitel is French-owned and the cuisine has a Gallic flavour (the '*bonjour*' and '*bonsoir*' greetings seem *une étape* too far, though). This might do for the local businessmen, but we prefer dining out as this is a superb location in Zona T – restaurants Casa (see p053), Central Cevechería (T 644 7766) and Di Lucca (T 257 4269) are on the doorstep. *Carrera 13 y 85-80, T 621 2666, www.sofitel.com*

Hotel Avia 93

As you sit on your 'Louis Ghost' chair in the informal reception of this 2010 hotel, first impressions are that it's surprisingly confident and contemporary. There's the tinted-glass building itself and, in the lobby (above), Leon Trujillo's silver-nitrate 'Milcilindros' chandelier, a dancing fire sculpture and a fine appreciation of space. Monochrome rooms are well proportioned, if slightly cold, with stone infinity showers or in-room baths for the uninhibited. But you'll wonder at some point if style might have triumphed over substance. Perhaps it's the glass walls that force you to lower the lumbering electric blinds (there are no views to speak of) or some flimsy finishing. Still, the Japanese restaurant IWAO is a bonus and Parque 93 is just a stroll away. *Calle 93 y 11a-31, T 705 1555, www.hotelavia93.com*

BOG
Nini Andrade Silva's simple yet opulent interiors infuse BOG with real sparkle, from the gilt-edged lobby and bar to restaurant La Leo (see p042) and the bronze, green and silver chromatics in the 55 rooms; Suite 801 (pictured) is the most covetable. There's even art by Olga de Amaral (see p030), sculptures by Hugo Zapata and a heated rooftop pool.
Carrera 11 y 86-74, T 639 9999

104 Art Suites

It's starting to look a touch outdated but the arty concept of Alejandro Castaño's pioneering 2007 project still makes this a worthwhile place to crash after a night in nearby Usaquén. Spread over six floors, the design of the 20 spacious suites was thrown over to promising young artists. Red chairs by Panton and the Eameses (opposite) and scarlet splashes on the facade tie it all together. Family Suite 503 (above), with its graffiti cat murals by Giovanni Sánchez, is our favourite. The owners have rolled out a similar approach at other venues, using jazz and celebrity as themes, and also operate Continental All Suites (T 606 3000) in Vicente Nasi's 1948 landmark, but missed a golden opportunity with a disappointing refit. *Carrera 18a y 104-77, T 602 5959, www.104artsuites.com*

24 HOURS

SEE THE BEST OF THE CITY IN JUST ONE DAY

Congestion and unpredictable weather are likely to be your only enemies on a typical Bogota day. So, if the sun's out, beat the traffic and take the cable car up to Monserrate (see po14). Downtown hosts the country's best museums – highlights are the veritable El Dorado on glittering display at Museo del Oro (see po26) and Fernando Botero's unmistakable bloated muses (see po28). Nearby, Espacio Odeon (Carrera 5 y 12c-85, T 743 7064) is just one of many fascinating private art spaces springing up in the city. Still within walking distance, Museo Nacional (Carrera 7 y 28-66, T 381 6470) provides an essential insight into the country's troubled history.

When travelling between districts, jump in a taxi – the lauded TransMilenio bus scheme has fallen victim to a lack of investment and petty crime. As evening approaches, you should head north. Drinking starts early, usually in a pub owned by the Bogota Beer Company, which provide refuge during *pico y placa*, the mayor's futile efforts to limit car usage at rush hour. The best places to rub shoulders with the *farándula* only get busy after 11pm, when the A-list have moved on from fine-dining areas such as Zona G (see po38). And if you're meeting Colombian friends, remember that planning doesn't figure highly here and improvisation rules, so stay flexible and go with the flow. Clubs close at 3am but the party rarely ends then. We don't want to see you home before dawn.
For full addresses, see Resources.

09.30 Centro Gabriel García Márquez

Colombia's Nobel Laureate, affectionately known as 'Gabo', left the country in the 1960s to settle in Distrito Federal, and it was actually the Mexican government that commissioned this cultural centre, library and gallery in Candelaria in honour of one of South America's most-loved authors. Rogelio Salmona's multilayered volumes form a swirling, free-flowing figure-of-eight that seems to weave in and out of the ancient street grid – only he could have worked such a tribute into Bogota's historic fabric just two blocks from Plaza de Bolívar (see p072). The Escher-like spaces frame delightful views of Cerro de Monserrate (see p014) and the terracotta roofs of the colonial houses. Take it all in over a coffee and a pastry in the café, courtesy of the ubiquitous Mr Juan Valdez. *Calle 11 y 5-60, T 283 2200, www.fce.com.co*

10.30 Museo del Oro

Bogota's jaw-dropping Gold Museum is the undisputed home of pre-Hispanic bling. It opened in 1968 in Germán Samper's concrete vault. Efraín Riaño's 2008 refit restored its lustre, notably in the stunning Sala de Ofrenda (pictured), an artistic interpretation of the gold-bathing exploits of Muisca chief El Dorado, a legend that fuelled Spain's 16th-century gold rush.
Carrera 5a y 16, T 343 2222

11.30 Museo de Arte

Enrique Triana set this contemporary art gallery back from the street behind a generous patio in a deferential nod to the Biblioteca Luis Ángel Arango (see p068) opposite. The monolithic block comprises two 46 sq m exhibition spaces and a large permanent collection that features Oscar Muñoz, Alejandro Obregón, Doris Salcedo, Beatriz González and Santiago Cárdenas. Triana's white box links to a neo-colonial building that houses the Museo Botero, also endorsed by Banco de la República. Its contents were donated by acclaimed Colombian artist Fernando Botero, and include 123 of his own paintings, as well as pieces by Picasso and Miró. A well-stocked museum store was added by architects Manuel Villa and Antonio Yemail in 2012. *Calle 11 y 4-21, T 343 1212, www.banrepcultural.org*

13.30 Harry Sasson

Few have done more for Bogota's culinary scene than Harry Sasson, whose drive to use only top-quality ingredients, grown locally, represents ground zero for local gourmands. He launched in 1995 in Zona T and followed with Balzac (T 610 5210), Club Colombia (T 249 5681) and Harry's Bar (T 321 3940). But it's this restaurant in a 1938 faux-Tudor mansion by Chileans Julio Casanovas and Raúl Mannheim, with a white-steel bird's-nest extension added by Sasson's brother Saul for its 2011 opening, that has the expense accounts, *politicos* and soap set hooked. Adding to the sense of occasion, Sasson is normally to be seen working in the open kitchen, and ventures out to meet and greet. Highlights of the understated but faultless menu are the ceviche, and scallops from the robata grill. *Carrera 9 y 75-70, T 347 7155*

15.00 Casa Amaral
Inspired by Colombia's pre-Hispanic and colonial past, Olga de Amaral paints intricate woollen weaves with gold and silver to make 3D pieces that now hang in both the Met and MoMA in New York. With sculptor husband Jim Amaral, she turned a Tudor-style mansion in Quinta Camacho into a studio/gallery. See her remarkable work in the attic (pictured).
Calle 69 y 7-28, T 210 1101

16.30 Salvo Patria

Ironically, finding a decent cup of joe is easier in London than in Bogota, as the world's finest coffee is mostly exported. Juan Manuel Ortiz travelled to Melbourne to learn the barista trade, and he and chef Sebastián Pinzón have created a perfectly formed hangout in hip Chapinero Alto. Pull up one of Natalia Martinez's PVC and wrought-iron chairs to watch Ortiz brew with mad-scientist paraphernalia and a stopwatch, using beans from Huila, Nariño or Quindio. If you don't bump into artists Mateo López or Nicolás Paris here, drop by their nearby studio, Cooperartes (T 248 2850), and also visit Mini-Mal (T 347 5464), for its cakes and art and design pieces, in one of the 1950s townhouses typical of this area (see p081).
Carrera 4a y 57-28, T 702 6367, www.salvopatria.com

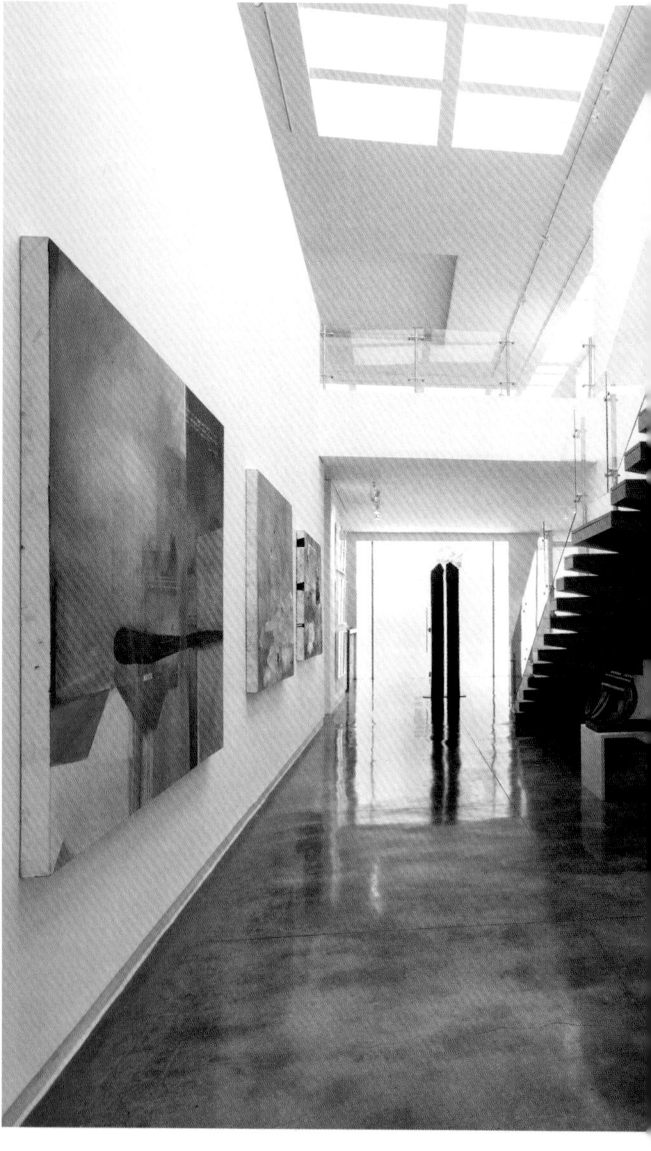

17.30 Galería La Cometa

Colombia's art scene is going through an exhilarating moment, which Serpentine Gallery director Hans Ulrich Obrist has likened to the explosion of Brit art in the early 1990s. Galeria Casas Riegner (T 249 9194) and La Central (T 757 4410) have both had great success showing young artists with an architectural background, such as Felipe Arturo and Gabriel Sierra. More established names, such as painter Luis Luna (opposite, left) and sculptor Edgar Negret (opposite, right) are found at La Cometa, a brick and concrete cube built in 2007. The gallery encompasses a café and a rear patio with sculptures by Jim Amaral (see p030) and Juan Jaramillo. A cantilevered wrought-iron staircase leads up to a floor where the family jewels are kept, including works by Fernando Botero and Santiago Cárdenas. Only for those with very deep pockets.
Carrera 10 y 94a-25, T 601 9494

20.30 Tábula

Facing the imposing walls of the Museo Nacional (see p024), which is housed in an 1874 panoptic prison, Tábula has been carved out of a Republican-style villa that dates from the same period. Architects and owners Juan Carlos Millán and Andrés Ortiz created a double-height dining area by wrapping the former garden with a steel frame supporting a translucent glass roof and laying down a raised deck; a living wall reconnects the space with the outside. The menu, by chef Tomas Rueda, is perfect for sharing, and includes hearty portions of lamb and beef slow-cooked for up to 10 hours in Tábula's wood-fired oven. Upstairs, El Libertador (T 245 1220) is a take on a 1950s New York bar. Next door, sister restaurant Donostia (T 287 3943) provides a taste of Spain.
Calle 29 y 5-90, T 287 7228

22.30 Magnolio

One of two perennially lively venues in Zona G run by Gero Basile and Mauricio Mancini, Magnolio builds on the success of Asian restaurant Kong (T 235 9229), and both attract a monied crowd from nearby Los Rosales. Magnolio's interiors accentuate the 1952 pedigree of its Tudor-esque residence and feature geometric wallpaper and plywood Eames chairs. But there's plenty of humour in the refit too, and the illuminated moose heads, snakeskin sofas and golden mirrored lions break the ice. See if you can blag your way up to the VIP floor, for its gentlemen's-club vibe and pool table, and to find out from the beautiful people where the after-party is. Basile and Mancini have a third celebrity-heavy hangout, Bardot (T 616 0029), in Parque 93.
Calle 69a y 5-19, T 211 0627

23.45 El Coq

Architect Felipe Rodriguez and a handful of creative partners blew the roof off the club scene in 2009 when they opened this 'imaginary' townhouse belonging to a Mr Coq. The strict filter applied at the door, plus the leather-clad walls and flocked wallpaper, contribute some elegance to the otherwise battered interiors. A bizarrely bandaged tree, a windmill and a door to nowhere add to the eclectic ambience but it's not so much the dream-like fixtures and fittings – or even the retractable roof that beats the smoking ban – that draws the city's trendsetters. An eclectic music policy shaped by fashion photographer/DJ Jorge Pizarro pits obscure Talking Heads remixes against indie classics and electro to ensure that El Coq continues to crow long after its rivals have come and gone. *Calle 84 y 14-2*

URBAN LIFE
CAFÉS, RESTAURANTS, BARS AND NIGHTCLUBS

A fraught history has taught Colombians to live every day as if it were their last, which has produced a high-octane existence and one of South America's most vibrant capitals. Bogota nightlife can be easily compared to a typical *sancocho* stew – grab whatever is to hand, add liquid and heat, stir for a few hours and enjoy the results. Indeed, the city itself is a melting pot. To name a few of its culinary VIPs, Harry Sasson (see p029) has roots in Barranquilla, Leonor Espinosa (see p042) is from Cartagena, Andrew Blackburn (see p045) is Scottish, Rafael Osterling (see p048) hails from Peru and the boys from El Botánico (see p054) are Spanish. Even blue-blood locals dining in refined Zona G don't know quite what to call themselves. 'Bogotanos' doesn't work. 'Cachacos' is a derogatory term used by their uncouth Caribbean cousins to denote an uptight guy in a suit. 'Rolos' is as close as anyone gets to a moniker they can live with. 'Nobody's from here,' is the common complaint, and yet it's the very mix of paisas, caleños, costeños and gringos that has created such an exciting, diverse and unpredictable scene.

What does unite them is an infectious zest for life. Nobody has yet bottled this unique Colombian spirit, but Andrés Jaramillo came close at Andrés Carne de Res (Calle 3 y 11a-56, Chia, T 863 7880), realising that Bogota's nocturnal activity functions as a pressure valve, an escape from the intensity of a tumultuous daily existence. *For full addresses, see Resources.*

La Mina

This superior surf 'n' turf restaurant was designed by the king of hospitality chic, Miguel Soto. For this low-lit eaterie in the JW Marriott (see p016), he took inspiration from the salt mine in Zipaquirá (see p096). Even before the Spanish caught a whiff of El Dorado, it was salt that persuaded them to settle in this mountainous terrain. Soto covered the arches of his 'mine' with a silver-plated copper mesh by Hechizoo

(see p086) – a choice typical of his no-expense-spared approach. Coloured salts from around the world accompany the dishes on chef Carlos Rivera's impressive menu, which includes New Zealand lamb, French truffles and lobster from Maine. The Italian wine list also keeps fat-cat expats happy as they tie up concessions for what remains of Colombia's precious resources.
JW Marriott, Calle 73 y 8-60, T 481 6000

Leo Cocina y Cava
Chef Leonor Espinosa's mischievous and colourful reinterpretation of traditional Colombian fare has been a revelation, her menu brilliantly reworking delicacies such as fried ants and yucca for an international palate. Noemí Pérez's large canvases on the walls are as bold as the flavours. Espinosa has a second restaurant in hotel BOG (see p020).
Calle 27b y 6-75, T 286 7091

Il Giardino

Usaquén's sophisticated culinary scene is largely down to restaurateur Leo Katz and designer Miguel Soto. In 2010, they injected some glamour into their Italian eaterie Café Amarti with an extra dining room, Il Giardino. The 'garden' occupies a former garage, its airy double-height space contrasting with Amarti's adjoining adobe interiors; a limestone floor and plenty of foliage add to the outdoor feel.

From the Italian marble bar, more than 20 varieties of fizz are dispensed to a smart Colombian set flaunting their new-found wealth. Next door is La Mar (T 629 2200), the Gastón Acurio ceviche franchise also from the Katz and Soto stable; the duo's other Usaquén ventures include the Luis Barragán-inspired meat-fest 7-16 (T 213 4271) and sushi bar Koi (T 213 3919). *Calle 119 y 6-24, T 214 9184*

Horacio Barbato

A back-to-basics formula of good-quality local ingredients cooked well has made this Usaquén restaurant a standout ticket for a sophisticated crowd. Scottish chef Andrew Blackburn's hearty cuisine fits like a glove with Bogota's inclement weather, and everything on the seasonal menu, from the homemade sausages to the shepherd's pie and the suckling pig, is cooked in a large wood-fired oven.

Architect Luis Restrepo played it straight, leaving much of the former colonial house intact, but he did incorporate a tree-lined patio shared with two sister restaurants. Next door, Osaki (T 644 7777) has earned a reputation for its excellent sushi, and 80 Sillas (T 619 2471) displays a similar no-nonsense approach to ceviche.
Calle 118 y 6a-37, T 644 7766,
www.horaciobarbato.com

El Bandido Bistró
Already ruling the roost with El Coq (see p039), Felipe Rodriguez and his team worked a French theme for this bustling evening haunt, which serves up bistro fare and live jazz. Eclectic interiors mix rescued classics by the Eameses with bespoke items by local designer Mariana Vieira. On a street famed for its antiques, El Bandido provides the final flourish.
Calle 79b y 7-12, T 212 5709

La Despensa

Peruvian chef Rafael Osterling imported his top Lima restaurant Rafael in 2007 and it was at the forefront of the invasion of sophisticated Peruvian cuisine. The airs and graces of his Bogota outpost (T 255 4138) in Zona G endear it to an older clientele of businessmen and sugar daddies; however, its hip younger brother La Despensa arrived in 2010. The classy cantina occupies a 1950s Quinta Camacho townhouse and offers a more rustic menu and low-key interiors; the unpretentious decor includes lamps made by Osterling's own design label, Dirty Dog. Reserve a table outside and kick off with a Pisco Sour mixed with lulo juice before tucking into the subtle Franco-Peruvian flavours found in dishes such as *pulpo a la griega*. *Calle 70a y 9-95, T 235 8891, www.rafaelosterling.com*

Astrid & Gastón

Gastón Acurio is the undisputed leader of the Cocina Novoandina movement, and Astrid & Gastón is the most distinguished arm of the Peruvian chef's empire. The cuisine here might not match the heights of Acurio's Lima original, but Colombian chef Francisco Rodríguez shows aplomb. No expense was spared in the upgrade of the 1932 Tudor-style mansion that houses it. Guillermo Arias provided the overall polished finish, big on sumptuous leather and mirrors. And Manuel Villa overhauled the house's ungainly extension, adding a perforated black-steel casing, boudoir lighting and velvet seating to create one of the city's most iconic bars (above). Beat the altitude with a Coca Sour and share some of the scintillating *tiraditos*. *Carrera 7 y 67-64, T 211 1400, www.astridygastonbogota.com*

Armando Records

Planted on the roof of a four-storey office block (which helped it get around the 2008 smoking ban), Bogotá's best live-music venue is the work of Edgar Morales and Bernardo Londoño of Meteoro Estudio. The club's popularity with hipsters prepared to queue around the block to catch imported bands that most of them have never heard of has served to catapult the city's other bars skywards. Armando has since doubled the size of its terrace and added the first-floor All Stars bar (pictured), which features a scarlet pool table, mirrored ceilings, refurbished 1960s furniture and a salsa soundtrack. There are plans to add a record exchange and recording studio when space becomes available.
Calle 85 y 14-46,
www.armandorecords.org

El Bembé

Check your coat and umbrella at the door and leave the changeable weather behind in this tropical paradise in La Macarena. The weekends start early at El Bembé, with a dancing matinee accompanied by live music from old-timers Los Tres de Cuba. In the evenings, the food's more filling than fantastic here, so eat next door at Leo (see p042) before slipping on your salsa spats. By 11pm, the house group will have the after-work crowd in a frenzy with their cha-cha-cha, charanga, boogaloo and more. As part-owner, the actress Ana Wills ensures that plenty of glamorous guests regularly climb El Bembé's spiral staircase to drill holes into the Cuban-themed tiles with their high-heeled spins.
Calle 27b y 6-73, T 286 0539

Casa

Guillermo Bermúdez was one of a group of great Colombian architects inspired by Le Corbusier's visit in 1949, and his family home is the finest example of his work. His son Alexander has converted it into one of the city's most sophisticated restaurants, with a modern European menu. The simple containerised form and the double-height windows that connect the living and dining rooms with an interior patio were influenced by Le Corbusier's plans for Citrohan House, and Casa is one of the few properties of the period rescued from the rampant onset of speculative towers. Book a garden table on a pleasant evening or, on cold nights, warm up in the bar, formerly Bermúdez's office, with a single malt by the open fire. In a nice touch, place mats feature the original blueprints.
Carrera 13 y 85-24, T 236 3755

El Botánico

A shortage of good restaurants in central Bogota led to a farcical situation in which the country's politicians would haul their cavalcades 100 blocks across the city and back at lunchtime to blow taxpayers' money in fancy eateries in the north. But those very same politicians allowed the roads to deteriorate so badly that they were spending most of their time stuck in traffic. Enter Juan Pedro and José Perez, the team behind lively venue La Puerta Grande (T 636 3425), with this restaurant/bar/club located in one of the colonial houses hidden behind the limestone-clad ministries that back on to the presidential palace. At weekends, when the bureaucrats head for their plush homes in the hills, El Botánico lures a happening crowd with international DJs and one-off parties.
Calle 6 y 7-33, T 289 7849

El Patio

Owner-chef Alejandro Bernal has been hosting left-leaning politicians and boho painters, filmmakers and journalists in his clandestine bolthole for two decades. Carved from a patio area in one of La Macarena's four-storey International Style apartment blocks, the restaurant was decorated by Bernal himself, collecting his clutter from the antiques stores that line Carrera 9 in Chapinero and the Sunday fleamarket behind the Museo de Arte Moderno (T 286 0466). Nothing matches. Not even the cutlery. The miscellany draws a dedicated crowd, as does the homemade pasta dishes and Mediterranean fare, and a soundtrack of Edith Piaf, tango and bossa nova. One corner of the seductive space is dedicated to former regular Jaime Garzón, a popular satirist who was shot in 1999. *Carrera 4a y 27-80, T 282 6121*

Criterión

Brothers Jorge and Mark Rausch come a close second (and third) to Harry Sasson (see p029) for the title of Colombia's most famous chef. Of Polish descent, they made their name through TV programmes and cookery books, but nothing compares to the enduring success of Criterión, the best French restaurant in the country. The 2003 minimalist interiors, by Orit Feldman, got a facelift in 2012 to give the venue a youthful appeal, including the addition of a pastiche of Banksy's Damien Hirst paintings in the bar/smoking area (right). On school nights and at lunchtimes, expense accounts mix with the ruling classes from Los Rosales, and at weekends, a special-occasion crowd gathers. Ignore the prices and order the Kobe beef Chateaubriand but leave space for the dessert-for-two, an edible work of art quite literally scribbled on to the table.
Calle 69a y 5-75, T 310 1377,
www.criterion.com.co

Abasto

Harry Sasson (see p029), Horacio Barbato (see p045), El Comedor (T 474 3847) and Abasto are the finest proponents of good, honest, locally sourced cuisine; the latter is the most affordable. Benjamin Villegas devised the menu of uplifting comfort food, from Bogota's best beef burger to a creamy prawn, chilli and avocado risotto. The interiors by Liliana Gutiérrez and Andrea Sánchez include red 'Marais A' chairs on the balcony and a rustic table by Pedro Londoño – grandson of architect Roberto (see p072) – that encourages communal convalescence in the deli area out back (above). Have brunch here on Sunday, explore the Usaquén fleamarket and see a matinee at the Luis Restrepo-designed Cinema Paraíso (T 215 5316), which even has tables for your drinks. Very civilised.
Carrera 6 y 119b-52, T 215 1286

Wok

One of the first Colombian food chains to champion sustainability and contemporary design, Wok also does great noodles and sushi. Guillermo Fischer created the first branch in Zona T (above) in 1998 and has been upping the game ever since. In 2003, he lifted the Avenida 19 outlet (T 213 8854) up on piloti, leaving a car park underneath. His 2008 addition (T 287 3194) on a more sensitive site adjacent to Thomas Reed's

Museo Nacional (see p024) uses bamboo shuttering to leave an Asian imprint on the cement exterior. In 2012, he added a third floor to the original, opening up an atrium lined with oak balustrades inspired by Finnish architect Alvar Aalto. Co-founder Benjamin Villegas (opposite) ensures Wok's Asian menu lives up to the interiors. *Carrera 13 y 82-74, T 218 9040, www.wok.com.co*

Matiz
Leonor Espinosa earned her stripes at
this upscale restaurant before going
solo (see p042). These days, it's Chilean
chef Nicolás Quintano who mixes cordon
bleu and Peruvian cuisine in the stylish
surroundings by Silvie Delesmontie.
The restaurant is named after legendary
Colombian snapper Leo Matiz, whose
black and white photos grace the walls.
Calle 95 y 11a-17, T 520 2006

INSIDER'S GUIDE
ADRIANA GALLEGO, HORTICULTURALIST

Founder of horticultural design studio Taller Vivo, Adriana Gallego lives in Candelaria, where she cultivates a secret garden and has an atelier. 'I love the city's creative energy,' she says. 'There's always something going on – it's electric.' To give her green fingers a rest, she strolls down to La Peluquería (Carrera 3 y 12d-83, T 320 864 4083), an avant-garde hair salon and bar in a colonial house. 'You meet interesting people there over a cuppa or a G&T.' When retail therapy is required, she heads to the showroom of Olga Piedrahita (Carrera 14a y 82-36, T 622 8681) to try out her inventive designs.

Gallego takes advantage of *ciclovía* – the closure of Carrera 7 to traffic on Sundays – to cycle to Usaquén. 'It's a charming village with a different feel to the rest of the city.' She likes to browse the stores selling organic food, designer objects and antiques, and eats at Abasto (see p058): 'They make the most amazing crumbles.' On a night out, she might dine at La Despensa (see p048), the petite Italian Julia (Carrera 5 y 69a-19, T 348 2835), which has 'the best pizza in town', or Wok (see p059) next to the Museo Nacional, especially if she's caught a show at Galería Christopher Paschall (Calle 22 y 5-88, T 282 4375). If friends are visiting, she'll reserve a corner of Andrés Carne de Res (see p040) for a blowout. There's now a second branch of Bogota's steakhouse institution in Zona T, yet Gallego insists: 'It has to be the original restaurant in Chía.' *For full addresses, see Resources.*

ARCHITOUR
A GUIDE TO BOGOTA'S ICONIC BUILDINGS

Unfortunately in Bogota, taking photos of buildings does not go down well with twitchy security guards. Much of rising star Daniel Bonilla's oeuvre, for example, has been commissioned by private clients. However, Fundación Rogelio Salmona (Carrera 6a y 26-85, T 341 6629) has recognised the interest in Colombian architecture and now organises tours of the city's seminal works.

Venturing out by yourself, stroll along Salmona's water-themed walkway, Avenida Jiménez, which ties together the best buildings that rose straight after the 1948 riots – Gabriel Serrano's Edificio Francisco Camacho (No 40), Bruno Violi's Edificio El Tiempo (No 93) and Germán Tejero de la Torre's Edificio Monserrate (No 49). Just off here is Parque Santander, home to the Museo del Oro (see p026) and the soaring 1968 Edificio Avianca (see p009).

On the city's other axis, 500 years of construction unfolds on Carrera 7, from the 16th-century Templo de San Francisco (Calle 16 y 7-35) to the shiny new towers of Calle 100. If you find yourself on the Circunvalar, take a detour into the city heights to see how the rich live. President Juan Manuel Santos grew up in Fernando Martínez's 1963 shapely brick creation, Casa Calderón (Carrera 4 y 86-21), and the 1969 Edificio Colinsa (Transversal 6 y 84-81) nearby has an oddly cantilevered corner – added simply to accommodate the giant dining table of Colombia's richest family (see p015).
For full addresses, see Resources.

Edificio Ayasha

Bogota has become far more welcoming towards international architects, which hasn't pleased the old guard but does sit well with the country's new-found global ambitions. This illuminated office block by Peruvian José Orrego typifies the trend. Contracted to add some chutzpah to an otherwise unremarkable office district in 2010, Orrego put on a show similar to that of Studio Pei-Zhu's Digital Building created for the Beijing Olympics. Formed by four slabs of black frosted glass that appear to float above a water feature, the LED motherboard motif takes commuters' minds off the chronic evening congestion. Go after dark but let the traffic die down by dining nearby at Pajares Salinas (T 616 1524), an old-money Spanish eaterie that's been pulling in *politicos* for two decades. *Transversal 21 y 98-56*

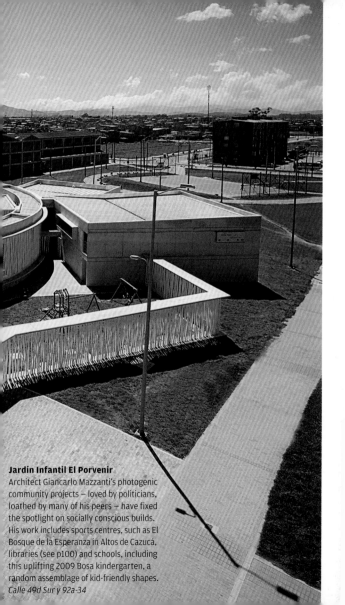

Jardín Infantil El Porvenir

Architect Giancarlo Mazzanti's photogenic community projects – loved by politicians, loathed by many of his peers – have fixed the spotlight on socially conscious builds. His work includes sports centres, such as El Bosque de la Esperanza in Altos de Cazucá, libraries (see p100) and schools, including this uplifting 2009 Bosa kindergarten, a random assemblage of kid-friendly shapes.
Calle 49d Sur y 92a-34

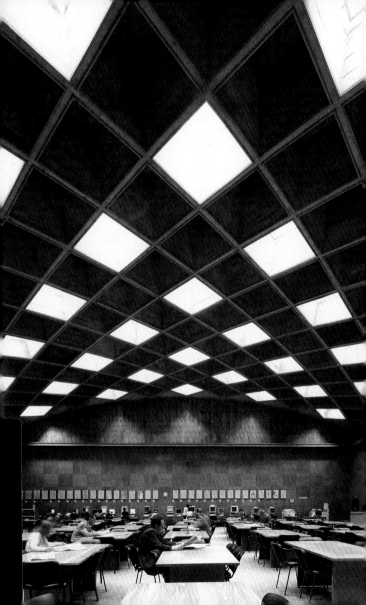

Biblioteca Luis Ángel Arango

This imperious cultural centre occupies an entire Candelaria block. It was constructed in two phases. From 1955 to 1958, architect Rafael Esguerra and engineer Doménico Parma created a lattice of concrete beams over the library reading room (opposite) to form a 28m-wide arched roof with 50 diamond-shaped skylights. Stored below is the largest collection of books in Latin America. Germán Samper added an oval music hall between 1965 and 1968, which remains the city's premier concert venue and possibly its most spectacular interior. Completing the building's singular attitude, a horizontal plane parts company with the sloping terrain, suspending one facade above the street (above), and provides a refuge from Bogota's regular downpours. *Calle 11 y 4-14, T 343 1224, www.banrepcultural.org*

Biblioteca Virgilio Barco

From 1995 to 2003, progressive mayors Antanas Mockus and Enrique Peñalosa put in place desperately needed citywide reform, including a series of parks and libraries linked by cycle lanes and public transport. Salmona's Biblioteca Virgilio Barco, opened in 2001, is arguably the city's finest example of public architecture. He submerged the monumental 16,000 sq m fossil-shaped structure below ground and added a semicircular moat to absorb noise from two adjacent highways. The roof sucks in daylight and its incline forms an open-air amphitheatre; the complex's spiralling walkways, inside-outside spaces and organic forms provide Salmona's trademark visual treats.
Carrera 60 y 57-60

Palacio de Justicia

During the 1980s and 1990s, drug-related violence stifled Colombian architecture and led to a proliferation of impenetrable blocks, gated communities and monstrous carbuncles. Not even the capital's political heart escaped. Roberto Londoño's Palace of Justice was razed after revolutionaries stormed it in 1985, and the awkward feel of its 1998 replacement (also by Londoño) is down to extra security measures. Three supersized sandstone-clad 'tables' jar with Fernando Martínez's subtle 1970 reworking of steeply sloping Plaza de Bolívar. At the rear, the building's 10-storey bulk hides better modern architecture on Calle 12, including Bruno Violi's elegant 1960 Edificio Quintana (No 14) and Obregón y Valenzuela's 1965 Banco Comercial Antioqueño (No 32).
Plaza de Bolívar

Universidad de la Salle

The bold expressionism of this university campus in the most elevated part of La Candelaria provides a stark contrast with the mainly single-storey 18th-century housing that surrounds it. Herbert Rauprich Jung's glazed stairwells were inspired by Erich Mendelsohn's Shocken Department Store in Stuttgart and are enduring symbols of the daring modern architecture that was built in the 10-year aftermath of the 1948 riots, which destroyed large pockets of the area. It's a Christian college, not open to visitors, but can easily be appreciated from the streets below. The hyperbolic arches of La Salle's Parroquia Nuestra Señora de la Estrella (Carrera 5 y 59a-44) also deserve a look, perhaps after a brew at the Antonio Yemail-designed Taller de Té (see p081).
Carrera 2 y 10-70

Museo de Arquitectura

Leopoldo Rother, one of the fathers of the modern movement, designed the 1948 printworks for Bogota's militant Universidad Nacional; 38 years later, the building was converted into a museum dedicated to his work. The main hall (pictured) hosts rotating exhibitions, and stored on-site are plans by Jose Valenzuela, Fernando Martínez, Vicente Nasi and Bruno Violi, all of whom contributed influential works to the campus, which can be viewed on a tour. You'll also see Salmona's Edificio de Postgrados, a 1995 study in patterned brick that became a prototype for the Biblioteca Virgilio Barco (see p070). Call ahead to check the students haven't locked the teachers out. We're not joking. *Carrera 30 y 45-3, T 316 5000 ext 16903, www.facartes.unal.edu.co*

Edificio Vengoechea

Perched jauntily in the north-west corner of the block occupied by Biblioteca Luis Ángel Arango, this building now houses the administrative offices of the cultural centre that engulfed it. Built in 1939, its construction was overseen by French architect Manuel de Vengoechea, but the sculpted balconies and circular columns probably owe much to his junior, Spanish architect Ricardo Rivas. The two split after completing this iconic apartment block, Rivas miffed at his mentor grabbing the glory. Vengoechea went on to design houses for Colombia's leading families, and Rivas left for Buenos Aires. In 1948, Vengoechea became mayor of Bogota, only to see the city go up in flames a month into his tenure after the assassination of presidential candidate Jorge Gaitán. *Carrera 5a y 11-68*

Casa Ensamble

Originally designed as a family home in 1958 by Alfonso Noguera, Luis Santander and Alvaro Larreamendy, Casa Ensamble is typical of the International Style found in La Soledad, a district blessed with wide avenues thanks to Austrian planner Karl Brunner. The building was converted into a theatre in 2008, and its unique interiors and furniture by Franco-Russian painter Anatole Kaskoff, who had been brought to Colombia in 1948 to help prepare for the Pan-American Conference, have thankfully been preserved. A kidney-shaped entrance space (above) is used for workshops and interval drinks. Other theatres of note include the 1935 art deco Teatro el Parque (Carrera 5 y 36-5) by Carlos Martínez, and Richard Aeck's Teatro Jorge Eliécer Gaitán (T 379 5750 ext 200), finished a year later.
Avenida 24 y 41-59, T 368 9268

Universidad de los Andes
Security is paramount at Bogota's elite
university but you can book an architour
of its hilly campus (see p064). Don't miss
the 1991 Edificio Alberto Lleras Camargo
by father-and-son Guillermo and Daniel
Bermúdez; Carlos Campuzano's 1998
library within Campito chapel; and the
sun-drenched pool at Felipe González-
Pacheco's 2009 Polideportivo (pictured).
Carrera 1 y 18a-12, T 339 4949

SHOPPING

THE BEST RETAIL THERAPY AND WHAT TO BUY

As Bogota became the kidnap capital of the world in the 1990s, its shoppers were a restrained breed. Now that security concerns are disappearing, they are starting to flash the cash, encouraging global brands to pile in around the Centro Andino mall (Carrera 11 y 82-71, T 621 3111); for something more authentic and unique, Olga Piedrahita (see p062) and Amelia Toro (Avenida 82 y 12-10, T 610 9296) are the country's two top designers. The antiques stores on Carrera 9 between Calle 60 and 69 are always good for a browse, as is the more high-end mix on Calle 79b between Carrera 7 and 9. Given the rise in the stock of Colombian artists, taking a punt on the work found at Cooperartes (see p033) and Estudio Las Nieves (see p082) could be the shrewdest investment you ever make.

Boisterous food markets have fed the city for centuries and many still function – the best preserved is Plaza de Mercado de las Cruces (Calle 1f y 4-60, T 289 9450), and Pasaje Rivas (Carrera 10 y 10) stocks artisan wares including crockery from La Chamba, elegant black clay pots and bowls that sit well in any kitchen. No trip to Colombia would be complete without scoring a kilo of its most energising export – coffee. Pick some up at La Bodega de Abasto (Calle 120a y 3a-5, T 620 5262), a more contemporary take on the Plaza de Mercado concept. It's located in Usaquén, which also provides the backdrop for the city's best weekend fleamarket. *For full addresses, see Resources.*

La Casa de Greta

This kooky boutique in a 1950s townhouse in Chapinero Alto is the brainwave of Laura Laurens. Her womenswear line marries the contemporary with a healthy vintage obsession, using bespoke fabrics printed and tailored in the upstairs workshop. She also creates limited collections twice a year. The integrity of the property has been preserved and its homely feel is enhanced by period and recycled furniture. Below, the Taller de Té (T 255 4128) was carved out of the garage by architect Antonio Yemail; the tea room is a popular hangout for the talented types who frequent this up-and-coming barrio. Also worth checking out are boutiques Mini-Mal (see p033) and Vintage Lab (T 300 572 6252), and restaurant La Guardia (T 345 9973). *Calle 60a y 3a-38, T 346 1445, www.lacasadegreta.com*

Estudio Las Nieves
An innocuous blue door is the gateway to
ArtNexus founder Celia de Birbragher's
conversion of a seven-floor textiles factory
into studios. She has gathered an exciting
group of artists – Saúl Sánchez (pictured),
Carlos Blanco, Camilo Villegas, Miler Lagos
and Guillermo Londoño – under one roof.
Persist in knocking, as the doorman and
his wife move slowly but surely.
Carrera 8 y 20-17, T 313 395 6679

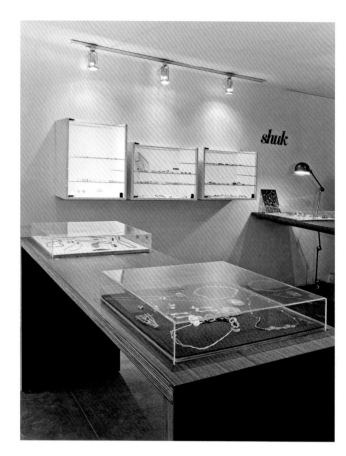

shuk

Mariana Shuk

The understated jewellery store/workshop of Royal Academy of Art graduate Mariana Shuk is located in a 1950s housing block. There's no sign – look for Taller Vivo's miniature gardens, cultivated by Adriana Gallego (see p062), hanging in the frosted windows. Shuk's uncomplicated, elegant jewellery has struck a chord with the low-profile mentality of the affluent inhabitants of this part of town – a certain paranoia about ostentatious shows of wealth being a hangover from the kidnap threat in the 1990s – and her subtle work with gold, platinum, silver and diamonds have won a loyal following. A keen collaborator, Shuk invites a designer or artist to join her in the workshop every few months, opening up the gallery space in her front room.
Calle 81a y 8-31, T 703 2735,
www.marianashuk.com

Loto

The essence of jasmine from the Andes and verbena from Argentina, and the scent of the acacia tree from the Amazon, are just some of the flavours trapped in a bottle by Johana Sanint's highly creative cosmetics brand. It's popular with the best hotels in town – Sofitel Victoria Regia (see p018) and BOG (see p020) carry Loto's hair and skincare products. The company opened this second 'delicatessen for the body' in the swanky Centro Andino mall in 2011. Designed by architects Octubre, the 1950s-style geometric tiling creates an old-school pharmacy feel – perfumes are dispensed from medicine bottles – given a modern slant with a custom-made steel lighting scheme. The colourful artisan soaps are wonderfully aromatic.
Local 149, Centro Andino, Carrera 11 y 82-71, T 703 5886, www.loto.com.co

Hechizoo
From two warehouses in the southern district of 20 de Julio, Jorge Lizarazo produces wonderful weaves, tapestries and rugs by combining traditional fibres with gold, silver, copper and PVC, and his work decorates many of the city's best hotels and restaurants. Perhaps pick up one of his cashmere hammocks. *Carrera 5 y 24a Sur 20, T 239 8644, www.hechizoo.com*

SPORTS AND SPAS

WORK OUT, CHILL OUT OR JUST WATCH

Acclimatise to the altitude before you slip on your running shoes here. Exercising at 2,600m can leave those not used to the lack of oxygen at Andean heights in a right state. Ease yourself in with a massage at Chairama Spa (see p092) before tackling Candelaria's hills with Bogota Bike Tours (Carrera 3 y 12-72, T 281 9924). Once settled, there's no excuse for not making the most of the largest network of cycle routes in Latin America – 300km of lanes created by former mayor Enrique Peñalosa to alleviate congestion.

Pedal west to Parque Salitre, a 55-hectare estate inherited by the government and now the city's most expansive green space. Parque Metropolitano Simón Bolívar is the place to join in a kickabout with the tippy-tappy locals. Nearby, you'll also find Bogota's top aquatic centre, Fernando Bonilla and Mario Motta's award-winning Centro Urbano de Recreación Compensar (Carrera 68 y 49a-23, T 428 0666), and the major sporting arenas. There's football at Estadio El Campín (see p094) and basketball, volleyball and table tennis in Jaime Camacho and Julián Guerrero's 1972 Unidad Deportivo El Salitre (Carrera 68 y 63, T 231 0762), a 7,000-seat indoor arena.

You'll need friends in high places to swim in Bogota's best pools, whether it's at the Universidad de los Andes (see p078) or in Jorge Arango's beautiful, glass-encased 1949 facility at the city's exclusive golf course, Country Club de Bogota (Calle 127c y 15-2, T 627 0155). *For full addresses, see Resources.*

El Cubo Colsubsidio

Financial companies such as Colsubsidio and Compensar (opposite) manage a mix of insurance, health and pension funds paid into by workers and employers, and have recently been competing to provide high-tech, eco-friendly sports facilities for their members. Colsubsidio commissioned Édgar Solano, Enrique Barco, Manuel Moreno and Javier Preciado to design a 32,000 sq m indoor centre, which opened in 2012. The main volume – a cube, hence the name – is all muscular steel struts and glass cladding, much of which is covered in a yellow mesh pattern. The seven-a-side football pitch (above), Olympic-size pool, 12 bowling lanes and putting green on the roof make it worth trying to get to know one of the 1.3 million people with access.
Carrera 30 y 52-77, T 746 5353, elcubo.colsubsidio.com

Plaza de Toros de la Santamaría
Ignacio Sanz de Santamaría donated the land and money to build this bullring and inaugurated a semi-completed 14,500-seat venue in 1931 but it soon bankrupted him. Spanish architect Santiago de la Mora added its Mudejar style in 1944. Mayor Gustavo Petro has taken a tough stance against the *corridas*; however the arena is also used for cultural events.
Carrera 6 y 26-20

Chairama Spa

It's surprising how few standalone spas there are in Bogota – considering the population's collective intake of toxic substances, you'd think that pampering palaces would be in high demand. It was only in 2010 that the capital got its first worthwhile wellness centre, a joint venture between former Miss Colombia Claudia Elena Vásquez, and architects Giancarlo Mazzanti and Plan B, who clad the four-storey building in modular steel, creating privacy without blocking out natural light. Chairama's exterior motif, and the treatments inside, are inspired by the culture of the indigenous Tayrona Indians. Gerard's beauty products add a touch of European-style luxury to the invigorating hydro-massage treatments. *Calle 95 y 11a-27, T 623 0555, www.chairamaspa.com*

Estadio El Campín

European architect Federico Leder Müller designed the 1938 Estadio Nemesio Camacho – affectionately known as El Campín, as it was built on a campsite. It's the home of the local football teams Millonarios and Independiente Santa Fe, as well as the national side; Colombia won the Copa América here in 2001. The capacity was expanded to 44,000 in 1950 after the arrival of legends like Alfredo Di Stéfano; the Argentine graced the stadium during a glorious spell at Millonarios from 1949 to 1953. Local architect Manuel Villa and Medellín-based Paisajes Emergentes upgraded the facilities in 2011. There are two seasons a year and games take place at weekends. Independiente were crowned champions in 2012 – the first time a team from Bogota had won the title in 24 years.
Carrera 30 y 57a

ESCAPES

WHERE TO GO IF YOU WANT TO LEAVE TOWN

The capital's frenetic nightlife can get to the most dedicated party animal. However, pristine beaches, deserted islands, picturesque coffee plantations and the Amazon rainforest are all less than two hours by plane. The Caribbean coast has been a playground for the rich ever since the Spanish arrived, and they left an impressive resort behind in Cartagena, many of its mansions now boutique hotels (opposite). There are also some stunning island retreats just off the coast that can be booked through Colombia Direct (Carrera 10b y 27-34, T 5645 8579), as can a trip to Parque Tayrona, a nature reserve five hours north-east, where wild beaches are backed by tropical foliage at the foot of the Sierra Nevada de Santa Marta.

Wealthy locals built weekend fincas lower down the mountain where it's much warmer. The best are two hours south, clustered around colonial Girardot, home to a market designed by Leopoldo Rother (see p074), and Anapoima, where Finca Basalto (T +1 631 731 1677, www.oasiscollections.com) is divine. If you are short on time, at least take in the remarkable Catedral de Sal (Carrera 6, T 852 9890) in Zipaquirá, where a series of chapels have been carved out of the hills. There's a daily train, or go by car to check out the former drug-baron's lair Castillo Marroquín (Autopista del Norte km21, La Caro, T 676 4101) – narcotecture at its finest. Stop for steak at Andrés Carne de Res (see p040) on the way back.
For full addresses, see Resources.

Casa Pombo, Cartagena

The walled city of Cartagena is a UNESCO World Heritage Site and a few of its colonial mansions have been turned into some of the hottest cribs in the Caribbean. The best are Hotel Agua (T 5664 9479), Sofitel Santa Clara (T 5650 4700) and Álvaro Barrera's clever conversion of Casa Pombo (flooded courtyard, overleaf), some parts of which date from the 16th century. The five suites mix contemporary and original features – 201 (above), with its enormous main salon facing the cathedral, is *the* place to entertain. There's a burgeoning culinary scene in town. We'd eat sushi at Tabetai (T 5664 4789) and grilled octopus at Donjuan (T 5664 3857), drink Mango Biche Mojitos at Malagana (T 5660 1360), and salsa at Quiebra-Canto (T 5664 1372). *Calle del Arzobispado y 34-14, T 5664 6286, www.casapombo.com*

Reflecting pool, Casa Pombo, Cartagena

Medellín

Two decades ago, Medellín was the murder capital of the world; these days, cable cars carry tourists to what used to be its most notorious barrios. The turning point was when politicians placed their faith in talented architects to create icons in the city's poorest districts. Biblioteca España (left; T 4385 7598), by Giancarlo Mazzanti, is housed in three monumental artificial rocks and has become the emblem of Medellín's transformation. Continue on the cable car to Parque Arví (T 4444 2979), a 70 sq km ecological site. Here, Felipe Uribe de Bedout added the Nucléo Comfama visitors' centre in 2011, which features subterranean chambers and giant flower beds; Uribe also created the popular Parque Pies Descalzos. The best place to stay overnight is The Charlee (T 4444 4968) – its Envy Suite has a jacuzzi and in-room teppanyaki grill. The rooftop pool and bar boast views over the city.

Casa Honda, Honda

Situated on the River Magdalena, Honda used to be the gateway to the capital for goods coming from the coast, but its strategic importance has waned. However, the sleepy colonial town, a three-hour drive from Bogota, still draws a weekend crowd. The architects of hotel BOG (see p020), Guillermo Arias and Luis Cuartas, built this escape in 2003. Occupying two formerly neglected colonial houses, the shells of which the architects retained, Casa Honda is spread over 1,400 sq m and features refined, contemporary touches, such as polished cement floors, steel girders and bespoke lighting. The various areas of the expansive whitewashed property are cleverly tied together by a pool and a patio lined with citrus trees. For availability, email the owners directly. *info@octubre.com.co*

NOTES

SKETCHES AND MEMOS

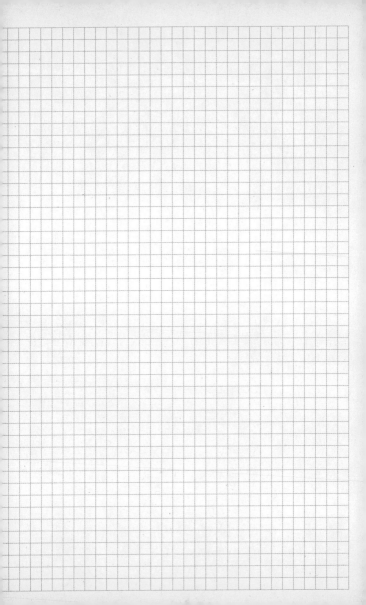

RESOURCES
CITY GUIDE DIRECTORY

HOTELS

ADDRESSES AND ROOM RATES

Hotel Agua 097
Room rates:
double, from US$380
Calle de Ayos 4 y 29
Cartagena
T 5664 9479
www.hotelagua.com.co

Hotel Avia 93 019
Room rates:
double, from US$210
Calle 93 y 11a-31
T 705 1555
www.hotelavia93.com

Hotel B3 016
Room rates:
double, from US$175
Carrera 15 y 88-36
T 691 8488
www.b3hotel.com

Hotel BH Parque 93 016
Room rates:
double, from US$150
Carrera 14 y 93a-69
T 743 2820
www.bhhoteles.com

Hotel Bioxury 016
Room rates:
prices on request
Calle 88 y 9-48
www.bioxury.com

BOG 020
Room rates:
double, from US$350;
Suite 801, US$430
Carrera 11 y 86-74
T 639 9999
www.boghotel.com

Casa Gaitán Cortés 016
Room rates:
double, from US$190
Calle 68 y 4-97
T 226 7247
www.loshotelesconencanto.com

Casa Honda 102
Room rates:
prices on request
Honda
info@octubre.com.co

Casa Medina 017
Room rates:
double, from US$420;
Junior Suite 406, from US$440
Carrera 7 y 69a-22
T 217 0288
www.hotelcharlestoncasamedina.com

Casa Pombo 097
Room rates:
double, from US$760;
Suite 201, US$2,250
Calle del Arzobispado y 34-14
Cartagena
T 5664 6286
www.casapombo.com

The Charlee 101
Room rates:
double, from US$195;
Envy Suite, US$385
Calle 9a y 37-16
Parque Lleras
Medellín
T 4444 4968
www.thecharlee.com

Cité Hotel 016
Room rates:
double, from US$280
Carrera 15 y 88-10
T 646 7777
www.citehotel.com

Click-Clack 016
Room rates:
prices on request
Carrera 11 y 93-77
T 691 9513

Continental All Suites 023
Room rates:
double, from US$115
Avenida Jiménez 4 y 16
T 606 3000
www.hotelcontinentalbogota.com.co

Finca Basalto 096
Room rates:
villa, from US$795 per night
(minimum three-night stay)
Anapoima
T +1 631 731 1677
www.oasiscollections.com

Hilton 016
Room rates:
double, from US$210
Carrera 7 y 72-41
T 600 6100
www.hilton.com

JW Marriott 016
Room rates:
double, from US$340
Calle 73 y 8-60
T 481 6000
www.marriott.com

104 Art Suites 022
Room rates:
double, US$140;
Family Suite 503, from US$210
Carrera 18a y 104-77
T 602 5959
www.104artsuites.com

Sofitel Santa Clara 097
Room rates:
double, from US$395
Calle Del Torno 39-29
Cartagena
T 5650 4700
www.sofitel.com

Sofitel Victoria Regia 018
Room rates:
double, from US$450;
Junior Suite, US$565
Carrera 13 y 85-80
T 621 2666
www.sofitel.com

WALLPAPER* CITY GUIDES

Executive Editor
Rachael Moloney

Editor
Jeremy Case
Author
Rainbow Nelson

Art Director
Loran Stosskopf
Art Editor
Eriko Shimazaki
Designer
Mayumi Hashimoto
Map Illustrator
Russell Bell

Photography Editor
Sophie Corben
Acting Photography Editor
Elisa Merlo
Photography Assistant
Nabil Butt

Chief Sub-Editor
Nick Mee
Sub-Editors
Marie Cleland Knowles
Emily Brooks

Editorial Assistant
Emma Harrison

Intern
Asha Aarti Mistry

**Wallpaper* Group
Editor-in-Chief**
Tony Chambers
Publishing Director
Gord Ray
Managing Editor
Jessica Diamond
Acting Managing Editor
Oliver Adamson

Contributors
Edgar Castellanos
Marta Devia
Pedro Franco
Eduardo Samper
Manuel Villa
Gregorio Von Hildebrand

Wallpaper* ® is a
registered trademark
of IPC Media Limited

First published 2012

All prices are correct at
the time of going to press,
but are subject to change.

Printed in China

PHAIDON

Phaidon Press Limited
Regent's Wharf
All Saints Street
London N1 9PA

Phaidon Press Inc
180 Varick Street
New York, NY 10014

Phaidon® is a registered
trademark of Phaidon
Press Limited

www.phaidon.com

A CIP Catalogue record for
this book is available from
the British Library.

ISBN 978 0 7148 6422 8

PHOTOGRAPHERS

Diego Amaral Ceballos
Bogota city view,
inside front cover
Casa Amaral, pp030-031

Rodrigo Davila
Jardín Infantil El
Porvenir, pp066-067

Juan Pablo Gomez
Casa, p053

Sergio Gomez
Edificio Aseguradora
del Valle, p010
Torre Colpatria, p011
Torres del Parque,
pp012-013
Santuario
Monserrate, p014
Edificio Bavaria, p015
Casa Medina, p017
Sofitel Victoria Regia, p018
Hotel Avia 93, p019
BOG, pp020-021
104 Art Suites, p022, p023
Centro Cultural Gabriel
García Márquez, p025
Museo del Oro del
Banco de la República,
pp026-027
Museo de Arte del Banco
de la República, p028

Harry Sasson, p029
Salvo Patria, p032, p033
Galería la Cometa,
pp034-035
Tábula, p036-037
Magnolio, p038
El Coq, p039
La Mina, p041
Leo Cocina y
Cava, pp042-043
Il Giardino, p044
Horacio Barbato, p045
El Bandido Bistró,
pp046-047
La Despensa, p048
Astrid & Gastón, p049
Armando Records,
pp050-051
El Bembé, p052
El Botánico, p054
El Patio, p055
Criterión, pp056-057
Abasto, p058
Wok, p059
Matiz, pp060-061
Adriana Gallego, p063
Edificio Ayasha, p065
Biblioteca Luis Ángel
Arango, p068, p069
Biblioteca Virgilio
Barco, pp070-071
Palacio de Justicia, p072
Universidad de la
Salle, p073
Museo de Arquitectura,
pp074-075

Edificio Vengoechea, p076
Casa Ensamble, p077
La Casa de Greta, p081
Estudio Las
Nieves, pp082-083
Mariana Shuk, p084
Loto, p085
Hechizoo, pp086-087
El Cubo Colsubsidio, p089
Plaza de Toros de la
Santamaría, pp090-091
Chairama Spa, pp092-093
Estadio El Campín,
pp094-095
Biblioteca España,
pp100-101

Andrés Valbuena
Universidad de los
Andes, pp078-079
Casa Honda, p102, p103

BOGOTA

A COLOUR-CODED GUIDE TO THE HOT 'HOODS

EL RETIRO/ZONA T
Smart boutiques share the streets with spirited bars and clubs in this gentrified zone

CIUDAD SALITRE
Beyond the vast campus of the Universidad Nacional lies Bogota's largest green space

DOWNTOWN
From the country's tallest high-rise to rundown markets, this is the city's chaotic centre

ZONA G/CHAPINERO
Many of Bogota's flashiest venues have been carved out of these 1930s to 1950s mansions

LA CANDELARIA
Museums, cultural centres and universities abound in the delightful colonial core

PARQUE 93/CHICO NORTE
The modern business district has a US feel in the bars and eateries around Parque 93

LA MACARENA
Students, artists and creatives have given this part of town a laidback, bohemian vibe

TEUSAQUILLO/LA SOLEDAD
All the mock-Tudor houses here could fool you into thinking you were in Middle England

For a full description of each neighbourhood, see the Introduction.
Featured venues are colour-coded, according to the district in which they are located.